BEFORE THE SETTING SUN

D0920837

TWENTY-MINUTE WORSHIP SERVICES FOR RESIDENTS
OF HEALTH CARE CENTERS AND RETIREMENT HOMES

Roger and Shirley Prescott

C.S.S. Publishing Co., Inc.

Lima, Ohio

BEFORE THE SETTING SUN: 20-MINUTE WORSHIP SERVICES
FOR RESIDENTS OF HEALTH CARE CENTERS AND RETIREMENT HOMES

Copyright © 1990 by
The C.S.S. Publishing Company, Inc.
Lima, Ohio

LIBRARY OF CONGRESS
Library of Congress Cataloging-in-Publication Data

Prescott, Roger, 1930-
    Before the setting sun: twenty-minute worship services for residents of health care centers and retirement homes / authors,
Roger Prescott and Shirley Prescott
       p.   cm.
    ISBN 1-55673-169-8
    1. Church work with the aged.   2. Worship Programs.   3. Retirees —
Religious life.   I. Prescott, Shirley, 1932-   II. Title.
BV4435.P74   1990
242'.86--cd20   89-27349
                                                      CIP

9016 / ISBN 1-55673-169-8   PRINTED IN U.S.A.

This book is dedicated to
The Residents and Staff
of
Bethany Lutheran Home
Council Bluffs, Iowa

Contents

Introduction

Grow old along with me!
The best is yet to be,
The last of life, for which the first was made:
Our times are in His hand
Who saith "A whole I planned,
Youth shows but half; trust God:
*   see all nor be afraid!*

— Robert Browning

I am always in hopes that our worship services can help make Browning's words live for our older citizens.

With this book in hand, and with about twenty minutes of thought and adaption, you ought to be able to produce a meaningful worship service for older people, one that will bring a word of encouragement and hope to your listeners — and makes you feel better about yourself.

We have had older people in mind as these thoughts have come together. They have been used and fine-tuned at the twice weekly services of Bethany Lutheran Home in Council Bluffs, Iowa. Our people here have received them warmly.

Furthermore, we have thought about the staff members too, always so helpful in gently getting people in and out — and pausing for some moments to participate also. More than once I have seen a nurse or aide stop and get caught up in a portion of the service.

Part of my philosophy in worship and Bible study with our older and frailer people is to use the same research intensity and illustrations I would use in the parish. Only with more brevity.

My wife, Shirley, has written the background to the hymns. I have had "more luck than sense" in life and most of it has been because of Shirley.

A Dutch writer/theologian sums up one of the purposes of this book:

We believe that aging is not a reason for despair but a basis for hope, not a slow decaying but a gradual maturing, not a fate to be undergone but a chance to be embraced.

— Henri J. M. Nouwen

9

We hope these services — and twenty minutes of your time to filter them through your mind and heart — will prove helpful to you and your people.

Roger and Shirley Prescott
231 Park Avenue
Council Bluffs, Iowa 51503

Some Uses for This Book

A helpful worship resource for:

- Nursing homes, retirement centers and hospitals,
- Women's, men's and youth groups,
- Personal and family devotions.

Visitors to hospitals, extended-care facilities and homebound people, will find these worship ideas helpful for a brief bedside visit.

Pastors and other speakers will find a source of illustrations to be mined.

The Lord's Prayer

Our Father, who art in heaven,
   hallowed be thy name,
   thy kingdom come,
   thy will be done,
     on earth as it is in heaven.
Give us this day our daily bread;
and forgive us our trespasses,
   as we forgive those
     who trespass against us;
and lead us not into temptation,
   but deliver us from evil.
For thine is the kingdom,
   and the power, and the glory,
   forever and ever. Amen

The Apostles' Creed

I believe in God, the Father almighty,
   creator of heaven and earth.

I believe in Jesus Christ, his only Son, our Lord.
   He was conceived by the power of the Holy Spirit
     and born of the Virgin Mary.
   He suffered under Pontius Pilate,
     was crucified, died, and was buried.
   He descended to the dead.
   On the third day he rose again.
   He ascended into heaven,
     and is seated at the right hand of the Father.
   He will come again to judge the living and the dead.

I believe in the Holy Spirit,
   the holy catholic church
   the communion of saints
   the forgiveness of sins
   the resurrection of the body,
   and the life everlasting. Amen

God's Strength

Welcome/Introductions

Invocation
This is the day which the Lord has made;
let us rejoice and be glad in it. (Psalm 118:24)

Hymn
"A Mighty Fortress is Our God"
Text: Martin Luther (1483-1546)
Tune: Martin Luther

About the Hymn
Martin Luther, the great reformer, loved music. He used music to spread teachings of the church and the Reformation. He said, "The devil hates music because he cannot stand gaiety. Satan can smirk but he cannot laugh; he can sneer but he cannot sing!"

Luther spent much time translating the scriptures into the language people could understand for themselves, and he wrote hymns in their language also. Philip Schaff notes, Luther translated the Bible into German "so God might *speak* directly to them in His Word," and compiled a hymnal "so they might directly *answer* Him in their songs."

During his years of struggle, Luther found an inner peace by meditating on the Psalms. Psalm 46 was the inspiration for this powerful hymn. Luther wrote both the words and the music. "A Mighty Fortress" testifies to the greatness of God and the ultimate triumph of God's truth. When Luther died, people lined the streets and sang as his casket was carried to its final resting place. The words are also engraved on the base of Luther's monument at Wittenberg.

Other hymns by Luther:
"From Heaven Above"
"Come, Holy Ghost, God and Lord"
"O Lord, We Praise You"

Scripture

God is our refuge and strength,
a very present help in trouble.
Therefore we will not fear though
   the earth should change,
   though the mountains shake in the
      heart of the sea;
  though its waters roar and foam,
   though the mountains tremble
      with its tumult.

               — Psalm 46:1-3
               (Full text: Psalm 46:1-11)

Special Music or Recitation (If any)

Sermon Seed

I heard about a tree in Oregon planted upside down. The branches were stuck into the earth and the roots were left up in the air. The tree grew well and did not die. The growing power within the elm tree turned the branches into roots and the roots into branches. The branches are gnarled and have the appearance of roots. The leaves are genuine elm leaves. The trunk is thicker at the top and would not be recognized as an elm by its base.

Some people are like this tree. With God's help, they adapt themselves to a changing situation even if their whole world is turned upside down by death, divorce, a life-sapping illness, an accident.

We admire the persons who keep the spirit of hope alive and growing, regardless of circumstances. They conquer their difficulties and accomplish their purposes in life in spite of adversity.

The Apostles' Creed

Prayer

Gracious God, we come to you today confessing our need to rely on your strength. We stand in need of your redemptive activity in our lives. We cannot create strength or faith in ourselves. They are your gift. Thank you for your promises and faithfulness. This we pray — and also as you taught us . . .

The Lord's Prayer

Hymn (Sing the last stanza of today's hymn)

The Benediction

The Lord bless you and keep you.
The Lord make his face shine on you
    and be gracious to you.
The Lord lock upon you with favor and
    give you peace.   Amen

God's Time

Invocation

This is the day which the Lord has made;
let us rejoice and be glad in it. (Psalm 118:24)

Hymn

"There is a Green Hill Far Away"
Text: Cecil F. Alexander (1823-1895)
Tune: Daman, Booke of Musicke, 1591

About the Hymn

When Cecil Frances was a little girl of nine, she began to write poetry. She was afraid to show it to her father, a stern military man, and hid the poems under a carpet! However, once her father discovered his daughter's talent, he set aside an hour each week to read what she had written aloud to the rest of the family. At the age of twenty-five she published her first volume of hymns for children. Although she married an English clergyman and became a wife and mother, she continued her hymn writing, producing more than 400 hymns. Most of her hymns were written for children. A child can easily understand them. But adults have admired her hymns over the years for their simple way of teaching the profound truths of our faith.

A few years before his death, her husband, Archbishop Alexander commented that he would be remembered not as an archbishop, but as the husband of the woman who wrote "There is a Green Hill Far Away."

Other hymns by Cecil Frances Alexander:
"Jesus Calls Us, O'er the Tumult"
"Once in David's Royal City"
"All Things Bright and Beautiful"

Scripture

But when the time had fully come, God sent forth his Son, born of woman, born under the law, so that we might receive adoption as sons.

— Galatians
(Full text: Galatians 4:1-7)

Special Music or Recitation (If any)

Sermon Seed

In the spring things turn green. We cannot rush spring, but have to wait. God's time is not our time. Patience is always needed. That includes things of the spirit.No one has put it better than one pastor:

I Remember

I remember helping
when I was very little,
helping two chicks
out of their shells
They both died.

I remember helping a rose to bloom;
it withered.

I remember pulling carrots
to see if they were ready,
then putting them back to grow.
They didn't.

I remember how hard it was to wait
for the fullness of time;
it still is.

But time always moves toward fullness;
it won't be hurried or held back;
it is God's very own creation
and all belongs to Him.

And that is good!

Gerhard E. Frost
Kept Moments
(Winston Press, 1982), p. 2

The Apostles' Creed

Prayer

Dear God in heaven, every day we are reminded of how fragile our lives are and how suddenly we may be summoned away from the things that engage us here. May the uncertainty of life make us more anxious to be faithful to our places in life while we have the opportunity. This we pray — and also as you taught us . . .

The Lord's Prayer

Hymn (Sing the last stanza of today's hymn)

The Benediction

The Lord bless you and keep you.
The Lord make his face shine on you
    and be gracious to you.
The Lord look upon you with favor and
    give you peace.
                                           Amen

Jesus

Welcome/Introductions

Invocation

This is the day which the Lord has made;
let us rejoice and be glad in it. (Psalm 118:24)

Hymn

"Stand Up, Stand Up for Jesus"
Text: George Duffield (1818-1888)
Tune: George J. Webb (1803-1887)

About the Hymn

This stirring hymn was written in response to the death of George Duffield's friend, Dudley Tyng. Tyng was a young pastor in Philadelphia in 1858. He was such an effective preacher that at a revival in Philadelphia he once had 1,000 people give themselves to Christ. A few weeks after this revival Tyng was watching a cornshelling machine. His arm was caught in the machinery and terribly mangled. As friends gathered around his bed, he asked them why they weren't singing and began to sing himself the words to "Rock of Ages." As he was dying, his father bent over him and asked if he had any last message for his friends. Tyng replied, "Tell them to stand up for Jesus!"

This message so impressed George Duffield that he preached a sermon the next Sunday from Ephesians 6:14 — "Stand, therefore, having your loins girt about with truth, and having on the breastplate of righteousness." He ended his sermon with the poem he had written, "Stand Up, Stand Up, for Jesus."

The poem soon found its way to a religious periodical and was set to a tune composed a few years earlier by George J. Webb.

Scripture

Put on the whole armor of God, that you may be able to stand against the wiles of the devil. . . . Stand therefore, having girded your loins with truth, and having put on the breastplate of righteousness, and having shod your feet with the equipment of the gospel of peace; above all taking the shield of faith, with which you can quench all the flaming darts of the evil one.

> — Ephesians 6:11, 14-16
> (Full text: Ephesians 6:10-20)

Special Music (If any)

Sermon Seed

Jesus Christ died for us. That's a basic part of our faith. We have been died for. There's a story that comes out of the South.

A young boy was working in the mills of North Carolina with his father. Suddenly the boy discovered that his clothing was caught in the machinery. He was slowly being pulled into the claws of a terrible, torturing death. He screamed in terror. His father, seeing what was happening, sizing up the situation in a glance, knew there was no time to run to the control room to shut off the power. He deliberately placed his own arm in the cog wheels to jam the machinery. The boy was saved but the father later died of infection from the severed arm. All the rest of his life the young man wore a red band around his arm. When people asked him why he wore the band, he would answer, "That is the mark of my father upon me. It reminds me that I have been died for."

> — Emphasis (C.S.S. Publishing Co.)
> October 1978, p. 18

We, too, have been died for. Therefore, we sing to remind ourselves to stand up for the One who died — Jesus the Christ.

The Apostles' Creed

Prayer

As we come before you today, gracious God, let your love come to us. Let your light shine in our hearts and minds that we might just naturally stand up for you as a natural part of our day. Soften our hurts and fears, and let a right spirit dwell within us. All this we pray, and also as you taught us . . .

The Lord's Prayer

Hymn (Sing the last stanza of today's hymn)

The Benediction

The Lord bless you and keep you.
The Lord make his face shine upon you
    and be gracious to you.
The Lord lift up his countenance upon you
    and give you peace;
In the Name of the Father, and of the Son,
    And of the Holy Spirit.   Amen

Steadfastness

Welcome/Introductions

Invocation

This is the day which the Lord has made;
let us rejoice and be glad in it. (Psalm 118:24)

Hymn

"Onward, Christian Soldiers"
Text: Sabine Baring-Gould (1837-1898)
Tune: Arthur S. Sullivan (1842-1900)

About the Hymn

Sabine Baring-Gould was a minister in England when he wrote this famous hymn. The children of his parish were to march to a neighboring church for a Sunday School rally on Whitmonday, 1895. "If only they could sing along the way, it would not seem so long," he thought. He searched for something suitable to sing, but found nothing. So he spent the greater part of the next night writing a hymn of his own, "Onward, Christian Soldiers." The next day the children's march was made lighter and happier by this great hymn. Baring-Gould often said later that he wrote it in such great haste that he thought some of the rhymes and meter were faulty. He would have been very surprised to know that today this "imperfect" hymn lives on while many of the 52 novels he wrote do not!

Objections are sometimes raised against the hymn because of its military spirit. A reading of the words, however, will show no hint of warfare with military weapons. The allusion is to spiritual warfare much as the Apostle Paul uses the imagery in the sixth chapter of Ephesians. The followers of Jesus are not to sit with folded hands and sing their way to heaven. Apostles and martyrs often sealed their faith with their life blood.

The Sunday School children of Baring-Gould's Parish sang these words to a different tune. "Onward, Christian Soldiers" has for the most part been inseparably linked to the tune by Sir Arthur S. Sullivan of the famous Gilbert and Sullivan team. He was a versatile musical genius. At the age of eight he could play nearly every kind of wind instrument. He composed his first musical piece at thirteen. He was an orchestra conductor, professor of music and church organist as well as a composer.

Other hymns by Baring-Gould:
"Now the Day is Over"
"Through the Night of Doubt and Sorrow"

Scripture

And the Word became flesh and dwelt among us, full of grace and truth.

— John 1:14
(Full text: John 1:9-14)

Special Music or Recitation (If any)

Sermon Seed

In Atlanta, Georgia, in the home of an Army Officer: On the first Christmas Eve following World War II, a woman answered the phone and heard her husband's voice. He had returned after several years overseas. You can imagine her happiness to hear the voice of her loved one, especially when she learned that he would be home for Christmas. He would be able to get home sometime during the night. They decided to keep his homecoming a secret from the children that he might surprise them on Christmas morning.

The next morning, when the children came down to see the tree and unwrap their presents lying beneath the tree, suddenly the white sheet on which the presents had been placed stirred, and up from among the packages arose their father!

Can you imagine the joy and happiness of that home? Expecting to find only presents, they found their father instead.

> — This story was told by Ralph W. Sockman in a sermon over the National Radio Pulpit on Christmas, 1946.

The Apostles' Creed

Prayer

Gracious God, we thank you for the blessing of steadfastness you have somehow placed in our hearts. And for the strength you give for the march of life. Christmas means that you are with us in our pilgrimage and so we have heart. This we pray — and also as you taught us . . .

The Lord's Prayer

Hymn (Sing the last stanza of today's hymn)

The Benediction

The Lord bless thee, and keep thee. The Lord make his face shine upon thee, and be gracious unto thee. The Lord lift up his countenance upon thee, and give thee peace. Amen

God's Nearness

Welcome/Introductions

Invocation

This is the day which the Lord has made;
let us rejoice and be glad in it. (Psalm 118:24)

Hymn

"Nearer, My God, To Thee"
Text: Sarah Flower Adams (1805-1848)
Tune: Lowell Mason

About the Hymn

Sarah Flower, born at Harlow, England, began and ended her life as a Baptist. During her adult years she was a member of the Unitarian congregation. She began a career on the stage, believing that plays (as well as preaching) could be made to teach great moral truths. Her dream did not materialize. She was forced to abandon her career because of poor health.

Sarah married John Bridges Adams, a civil engineer, and lived the rest of her life in London. She discovered her literary talent. Her sister, Eliza, was a musician who put Sarah's words to music. They published a hymn book, *Hymns and Anthems* in 1841.

One of the hymns contained in that book was "Nearer, My God, to Thee." Sarah had written the words while caring for Eliza who had tuberculosis, and after reading the story of Jacob at Bethel in Genesis 28:10-22. The tune we know was later written by Lowell Mason.

Sarah Adams died soon after her sister, also from tuberculosis. Although she did write other hymns, she is remembered as the author of "Nearer, My God, to Thee."

27

The hymn has been criticized because it does not speak of Christ and has been called "more Unitarian than Christian." Some theologians have to update the words to make the hymn "more Christian." None has been able to match the popularity of the original. It was a favorite of President William McKinley. As he lay dying of an assassin's bullet, his doctor heard him murmur "Nearer, My God, to Thee, Nearer to Thee." It is said that the Titanic's orchestra also played this hymn the night the great vessel sank.

Scripture

God is our refuge and strength, a very present help in trouble. Therefore we will not fear though the earth should change, though the mountains shake in the heart of the earth.

— Psalm 46:1-2
(Full text: Psalm 46:1-11)

Special Music or Recitation (If any)

Sermon Seed

The nearness of God is revealed each day by the wonders of nature around us. When we look closely we can see and feel God's presence in the animals and foliage of the earth. One writer gives us an image of the links between nature, humanity and God.

Maturity

Our little maple,
just four feet tall two years ago
but today I saw my first bird
perch briefly
among her branches.

So now our tree is more than a tree;
she is connected, she has reached out,
offered herself to a universe of needs.
She's promise, shelter, resting-place;
she offers habitat.

So with us, too, the family
of humankind.
We're meant to offer homes
to one another
as confidants and burden-sharers.
This is maturity.

> — Gerhard E. Frost
> *This Land of Leaving*
> (Shepherd's Staff Publications, 1986)

The Apostles' Creed

Prayer

Heavenly Father, we feel your nearness now. Grant us the
serenity to accept the things we cannot change, the courage to
change the things we can, and the wisdom to know the differ-
ence. Comfort us in your nest of nature. This we pray — and
also as you taught us . . .

The Lord's Prayer

Hymn (Sing the last stanza of today's hymn)

The Benediction

The Lord bless you, and keep you.
The Lord make his face shine on you
    and be gracious to you.
The Lord look upon you with favor and
    give you peace. Amen

Thanksgiving/Gratitude

Welcome/Introductions

Invocation

The Lord is in his holy temple; let all the earth keep silence before him. (Habakkuk 2:20)

Hymn

"Now Thank We All Our God" (Sing first stanza)

About the Hymn

Text: Martin Rinkhart (1586-1649)

Martin Rinkhart (1586-1649) was born in Eilenburg, Saxony in Germany in 1586. He attended school in his home town and then the University of Leipzig. In 1617, by invitation of the town council, he became the pastor of the church in the city of his birth at the beginning of the Thirty Years' War.

Because Eilenburg was a walled city, thousands of refugees swarmed in the city. The other two pastors in the city died and Rinkhart was the only pastor. He was sometimes called on to bury up to forty or fifty people on some days. One year, 8,000 persons, including Rinkhart's wife, died in Eilenburg. In this time of suffering and personal heartbreak, he wrote hymns of praise and thanksgiving. His most famous hymn is "Now Thank We All Our God."

Perhaps no hymn except Luther's "A Mighty Fortress" has been more generally used in the Lutheran Church. In Germany, it was sung at all impressive occasions; at the opening of the Cathedral of Cologne and the cornerstone laying at the Parliament Building in Berlin. It was sung in England by nearly all churches and chapels at the close of the Boer War in 1902.

Scripture

O give thanks to the Lord, for he is good;
for his steadfast love endures forever!
(Psalm 107:1)

. . always and for everything giving thanks in the name of
our Lord Jesus Christ to God . . .
(Ephesians 5:20)

Special Music (If any)

Sermon Seed

Today's hymn can help us develop an attitude of gratitude.
Martin Rinkhart could give thanks even in the face of over-
whelming tragedy. We, too, can learn and develop that attitude also. We could start by giving thanks for the unlikely
events called "forgetfulness." A poet/theologian helps us in
that regard:

I forgot my glasses today,
left them at the home of a friend.
I went to get them, forget my hat,
went to pick up the hat. On the way
I met an old acquaintance, remembered
the face but forgot the name!

I looked for an excuse.
"I'm old," I sighed, "old, old, old!"
and I was angry and sad.
Then I remembered some things
I'd forgotten I knew:

Forgetfulness is a gift, one of
the best from our gift-giving God.
Without it, what would I do?
I'd be unfit for each day's journey,
crushed by the past, broken under
an unbearable load.

31

So, dear God, guide me into forgetting;
help me to let go.
Make me always ready to relinquish
the painful baggage of yesterday — the
slurs and slaps, the burns and bruises.
School me in purposeful forgiving
and forgetting as I grow old.

—Gerhard E. Frost
"Deep in December"
Logos Art Productions

The Apostles' Creed

Prayer

We thank thee, O God, for the presence of your spirit with us now. And for the remembrance of the life of Jesus that once was lived out on this common earth under these ordinary skies. This we pray, and also as you taught us . . .

The Lord's Prayer

Hymn (Sing the last stanza of today's hymn)

The Benediction

Go in peace and serve the Lord.

Hope/Christmas

Welcome/Introductions

Invocation
The Lord is in his holy temple; let all the earth keep silence before him. (Habakkuk 2:20)

Hymn
"O Little Town of Bethlehem"
Text: Phillips Brooks (1835-1893)
Tune: Lewis H. Redner (1831-1908)

About the Hymn
    Phillips Brooks was an Episcopalian bishop and pastor of Holy Trinity Church in Boston. People came from all over the world to hear him preach. Brooks was also a gifted poet and loved the hymns of the church. By the time he started college he had memorized more than 200 hymns. He also loved children. One Christmas season, he wanted to do something special for the children of his Sunday School. He decided to write a poem about his experience a few years earlier when he visited Bethlehem.

    He quickly wrote the words and gave them to his Sunday school superintendent, Lewis Redner, to set to music. Redner waited for an inspiration for a suitable melody, but none seemed to come. On Christmas Eve he went to bed without having written a tune. Then, during the night, he was "awakened by an angel strain," as he later told it. He quickly wrote down the melody, went back to sleep, finished harmonizing the carol in the morning and taught it to the Sunday school children on Christmas Day, 1868. Redner always insisted the tune was "a gift from heaven." Many who sing it today agree.

Another hymn by Brooks:
"God Hath Sent His Angels"

Scripture

And all went to be enrolled, each to his own city. And Joseph also went up from Galilee, from the city of Nazareth, to Judea, to the city of David, which is called Bethlehem . . .

— Luke 2:3-4
(Full text: Luke 2:1-14)

Special Music (If any)

Sermon Seed

Here is a wonderful and tender Christmas story that comes out of the world of children:

It happened in a children's Christmas play. The time came for Mary and Joseph to ask for a room in the Inn. The boy playing the innkeeper was prompted to say, "No! Begone! We have no room in the Inn."

Joseph put his arm around Mary and they started to leave to find lodging somewhere else. Watching the forlorn couple, the boy's mouth opened. His brow was ceased with concern. His eyes filled with tears and he called after them, "Don't go, Joseph! Bring Mary back." And with a smile, he continued, "You can have my room!"

Children really get involved in what they do, don't they? And until they learn differently from some mob models, they are generally wonderfully kind.

The Apostles' Creed

Prayer

O God, the wonder of your life and love in the birth of Jesus fills us with awe. We are thankful that your actions are mysterious and we are constantly reminded that we don't know it all. Help us to remain open to the power of your presence, and keep us thinking like children. May our compassion be freed up to move out into the world of need. All this we pray, and also as you taught us . . .

The Lord's Prayer

Hymn (Sing the last stanza of today's hymn)

The Benediction

The Lord bless you, and keep you.
The Lord make his face shine upon you,
    and be gracious unto you.
The Lord lift up his countenance upon you,
    and give you peace;
In the Name of the Father, and of the Son,
    and of the Holy Spirit. Amen

The Need and Nearness of God

Welcome/Introductions

Invocation

This is the day which the Lord has made;
let us rejoice and be glad in it. (Psalm 118:24)

Hymn

"I Need Thee Every Hour"
Text: Anne Sherwood Hawks
Tune: Robert Lowery

About the Hymn

Anne Sherwood Hawks was a homemaker going about her daily tasks in April 1872, when she was filled with the sense of the presence of God and the assurance that he was near both in joy or in pain. She later wrote the poem, "I Need Thee Every Hour," that day. Later, she showed the poem to her pastor, Robert Lowry, a noted composer. He recognized the potential of the words and composed the melody to which it is still sung today. Mrs. Hawks wrote more than 400 hymn-poems during her life, but this one, with its sincere expression, dependence on God for wisdom and strength every hour of the day, is the one that has survived.

Gospel hymns of this type are often criticized by musicians and theologians for sentimental melodies and texts that are superficial and lacking in doctrine, but they continue to be sung and loved by many. Some assert that their obviousness is their strength — where delicacy and dignity make no impression, the gospel hymn stands up triumphant.

Scripture

Out of the depths have I cried unto
   thee, O lord.
Lord, hear my voice; let thine ears
be attentive to the voice of my
   supplications.

> — Psalm 130:1-2
> (Full text: Psalm 130:1-8)

Special Music or Poetry (If any)

Sermon Seed

A man and a woman were driving from Bemidji to Minneapolis to begin a three-day "second honeymoon" celebrating their twenty-fifth wedding anniversary.

As they moved along at the fifty-five m.p.h. speed limit they came upon a beat-up old clunk just barely cruising at about forty m.p.h. Two young were people in it, a boy and a girl, close together, obviously much in love.

"Walter," said Eleanor, "Why don't we ever sit together like that anymore?"

Walter kept his eyes straight ahead, his hands firmly on the wheel and quietly said, "I haven't moved."

We smile at that. We can draw a point from it. If we have moved away from a close relationship with God, the source of our life and strength — guess who has moved.

The Apostles' Creed

Prayer

O God — steer our straying thoughts toward you. We need your guidance always. Calm within us our restless spirits. Gather up the loose threads of our lives and weave them into a new tapestry of your design. Stick as close to us as glue, and create in us new spirits. All this we pray, and also as you taught us . . .

The Lord's Prayer

Hymn (Sing the last stanza of today's hymn)

The Benediction

The Lord bless you, and keep you.
The Lord make his face shine upon you,
    and be gracious unto you.
The Lord lift up his countenance upon you,
    and give you peace;
In the Name of the Father, and of the Son,
    and of the Holy Spirit. Amen

The Wonder and Power of Nature

Welcome/Introductions

Invocation

This is the day which the Lord has made;
let us rejoice and be glad in it. (Psalm 118:24)

Hymn

"Rock of Ages"
Text: August M. Toplady (1740-1778)
Tune: Thomas Hastings (1784-1872)

About the Hymn

August Toplady was ordained as a minister of the Church of England when he was twenty-two. Once while traveling through Somersetshire, England, he found himself in a terrible storm. He took shelter in a great cleft rock in Burrington Gorge. While waiting for the storm to subside, the idea for this great hymn came to him. It was later published in "The Gospel Magazine," a religious paper which he edited. Toplady died of tuberculosis two years later.

"Rock of Ages" often turns up in surveys of religious hymns as the favorite of many people. It was a favorite of Queen Victoria and Prince Albert. In the closing moments of Prince Albert's life, he was heard to repeat the famous lines. The hymn has been translated into almost every known language. On the 100th anniversary of the hymn, more than 10,000 people gathered at the place where it was supposed to have been written to pay homage to this great symbol of faith, expressed in song.

Scripture

God is our refuge and strength, a very present help in trouble. Therefore we will not fear though the earth should change, though the mountains shake in the heart of the sea; though its waters roar and foam, though the mountains tremble with its tumult.

— Psalm 46:1-3

Special Music (If any)

Sermon Seed

More than one hundred years ago a Frenchman — Fizeau, found a way to measure the speed of light. He found it to be 186,000 miles per second. That's a distance equal to seven times around the earth per second. Amazing!

In 1886 Heinrich Hertz demonstrated that radio waves travel at the same speed as light.

These discharges made possible the development of R-A-D-A-R, an abbreviation of the words "radio detection and ranging." This determination of a distance involves the accurate measurement of time in millionths of a second. Radio and light waves travel about 1,000 feet per millionth of a second. For instance if the object is ten miles away, approximately 50,000 feet, it takes 100-millionths of a second for the radio signal to go out and back. This time is measured by the use of a cathode ray tube, a standard piece of apparatus in most laboratories.

This is just one small example of the wonder and orderliness of creation. Our faith truly looks up to God when we see such wonderful and mighty things as this — and the majesty of the human mind which can discover them.

The Apostles' Creed

Prayer

O God — in the beginning you created all things. — Space and time and material substance. — All things that creep and fly, swim and walk. Let us stand today for all that is pure and true and just and good. And let us use our minds in concert with your majestic laws. This we pray and also as you taught us . . .

The Lord's Prayer

Hymn (Sing the last stanza of today's hymn)

The Benediction

Go in peace and serve the Lord.

The Holiness of Creation

Welcome/Introductions

Invocation
This is the day which the Lord has made;
let us rejoice and be glad in it. (Psalm 118:24)

Hymn
"Holy, Holy, Holy" (Sing first stanza)
Text: Reginald Heber (1783-1826)
Tune: John B. Dykes (1823-1876)

About the Hymn

Reginald Heber was born in Cheshire, England, and educated at Oxford, where he became a friend of Sir Walter Scott. Heber's gift for writing poetry was evident at that time. At seventeen, he wrote a poem on Palestine, read it to Scott, who suggested a closing line for it. The poem won a prize that Heber had been seeking.

He served for sixteen years in an obscure parish in the village of Hodnet. It was during this time that his fifty-seven hymns were written, although many of them were not published until after his death. Some of his hymns reveal the intense missionary fervor and secret longing he had to serve in India. His prayers were answered, when in 1822, he was appointed Bishop of Calcutta. He served there, with distinction, for four years. His life ended tragically when, after preaching to a large audience, he went for a swim in a friend's pool, was seized by a stroke and drowned. He was forty-three.

"Holy, Holy, Holy" was written by Heber especially for Trinity Sunday. It is based on the text from Revelation 4:8. The beautiful language of this hymn has made it a favorite of many. It is a hymn of pure adoration. It contains nothing of confession, petition or thanksgiving. Among the hymn's admirers was Alfred Lord Tennyson, who called it the world's greatest hymn! It is also a tribute to Heber that almost all of his fifty-seven hymns are still in use today.

The composer, John B. Dykes, was also an English clergyman. He wrote more than 300 hymn tunes and was one of the first to compose a melody to fit certain words. Before this, words and music were often printed in different books and the same melody would often be used with several different texts.

Scripture
Holy, holy, holy, is the Lord God Almighty.
— Revelation 4:8

The earth is the Lord's and the fulness thereof, the world and those who dwell therein; For God has founded it upon the seas, and established it upon the rivers.
— Psalm 24:1-2

Special Music (If any)

Sermon Seed
The Psalmist declares that everything belongs to and is created by God. Today's hymn speaks about giving praise to God for the richness of heaven and earth. "Holy, Holy, Holy" is not only a tribute to the Trinity, but music of reverence and awe. I see it as a hymn of adoration of nature as well as worship of our Creator. A line from the fourth stanza, "All Thy works shall praise Thy Name," helps us to see God in the ordinary things of the earth. Nature for instance:

Climb the mountains and get their good tidings. Nature's peace will flow into you as sunshine flows into trees. The winds will blow their freshness into you, and the storms their energy, while cares will drop off like falling leaves.

— John Muir
From a banner in a
church in Western
North Dakota

43

The Apostles' Creed

Prayer

O God — help us to go forth each day into Your world with a brave and trustful heart. And help us to understand our destiny as children of Thee. Amidst the changes and chances of life give us insight to see You hidden in all of creation. Let us use this world, but not abuse it. This we pray, and also as you taught us . . .

The Lord's Prayer

Hymn (Sing the last stanza of today's hymn)

The Benediction

May God bless you and keep you.
May God's face shine on you
    and be gracious to you.
May God look upon you with favor and
    give you peace.

Adoration of Christ

Welcome/Introductions

Invocation

This is the day which the Lord has made;
let us rejoice and be glad in it. (Psalm 118:24)

The Lord is in his holy temple; let all the earth keep silence
before him. (Habakkuk 2:20)

Hymn

"Beautiful Savior"

About the Hymn

While every hymn has a story, sometimes the origin is obscure and difficult to trace. Legends grow up around some of our favorite humns and become generally accepted. This is the case for "Beautiful Savior."

In many older hymnbooks, this lovely hymn is called the "Crusaders' hymn" and was said to have been sung by German knights on their way to Jerusalem.

Actually, it is a much newer hymn. It first appeared anonymously in 1677 and it was not until 1842 that it appeared with the present tune. It was explained that both the text and tune were taken down from oral recitation in the district of Glaz, in lower Silesia. Folk music such as this is by definition communal in nature, without known composers, but with strong national characteristics.

The English translation of "Beautiful Savior" comes to us by Joseph A. Seiss, a Lutheran preacher from Philadelphia.

Scripture

And in that region there were shepherds out in the field, keeping watch over their flock by night. And an angel of the Lord appeared to them, and the glory of the Lord shone around them, and they were filled with fear. And the angel said to them, "Be not afraid; for behold, I bring you good news of a great joy which will come to all the people; for to you is born this day in the city of David a Savior, who is Christ the Lord."

— Luke 2:8-11

Special Music (If any)

Sermon Seed

There was once a little girl who did not want to be left alone when she was put to bed. She wanted someone to sit with her.

"You've got your doll," said her mother. "Your doll will keep you company."

"When I'm lonely," said the little girl, "a doll is no good to me. I want someone with skin on her face."

That's a great response, isn't it? When we are lonely or frightened, we like real people beside us.

Maybe this little story will help us to think of poor people, old people, refugee people and other lonely people. They too want more than our words. They want the love and friendship of real people.

Remember, our Lord said, "Inasmuch as you did it unto the least of these, my brethren, you did it unto me."

The Apostles' Creed

Prayer

O God — beautiful Savior, steer our straying thoughts toward you. Calm within us the troubled spirit which often loses sight of your wonder. Gather up the loose strands of our lives and sew them into a new garment of meaning for each one of us. In this moment begin anew your work within us as we search for your will for our lives. This we pray, and also as you taught us . . .

The Lord's Prayer

Hymn (Sing the last stanza of today's hymn)

The Benediction

The Lord bless you, and keep you.
The Lord make his face shine upon you,
    and be gracious unto you.
The Lord lift up his countenance upon you,
    and give you peace;
In the name of the Father, and of the Son,
    and of the Holy Spirit. Amen

Trust

Welcome/Introductions

Invocation

The Lord is in his holy temple; let all the earth keep silence before him. (Habakkuk 2:20)

Hymn

"Blessed Assurance"

Text: Fanny Crosby (1820-1915)
Tune: Mrs. Joseph F. Knapp

About the Hymn

Fanny Crosby (1820-1915) was an amazing woman. She lost her sight when she was an infant because of faulty medical treatment. However, blindness did not stop her from leading a rich, full life. When she was fifteen she entered the Institute for the Blind in New York City. There she began to develop her poetic talents. At first she wrote only secular songs. In fact it was not until she was forty-one years old that she began to write hymns. Feeling that she had found her real mission in life, she continued writing hymns (nearly 8,000!) until her death at ninety-five.

Once when she was a guest of Mr. and Mrs. Joseph F. Knapp, one of the founders of Metropolitan Life Insurance, Mrs. Knapp asked Fanny to listen to a new melody she had composed. She asked "What do you think this tune says?" and immediately Fanny Crosby answered, "Blessed assurance, Jesus is mine!" In just a few minutes, the famous hymn was born. Critics have said that Fanny Crosby wrote too many hymns and too quickly and that many were not of high poetic quality. However, today we still have many lovely and much loved hymns written by a cheerful and confident Christian woman. Her life as well as her hymns have been an inspiration to many.

48

Scripture

Now faith is the assurance of things hoped for, the conviction of things not seen. . . . By faith we understand that the world was created by the word of God, so that what is seen was made out of things which do not appear.

— Hebrews 11:1, 3

Special Music (If any)

Sermon Seed

After an exceptionally heavy snowstorm a father and his young son were out riding in an automobile. "Look at those elm trees," commented his father. "The branches are so badly broken that it is quite likely the trees will die. But now look at those evergreens. The snow hasn't damaged them at all."

He continued, "There are two kinds of trees in the world — the stubborn and the wise. The elm tree holds its branches rigid and troubles pile on it until finally its limbs break, disfiguring the trees or killing it. But when the evergreen is loaded with more weight than it can hold, it simply reflexes, lowers its branches, and lets the burdens slip away. The evergreen is unharmed."

Then the father turned to his child and said, "Be like the evergreen tree, son, bear what you can and let the rest of the load slide off. You will live longer and have more life besides."

But there are certain troubles, handicaps, and hardships that we have to live with — like the thorn in the flesh to which St. Paul refers. If we seek God's will in our lives, we shall learn how even these things can be used for good.

— Roger Prescott
Hello, My Friend
(C.S.S., 1981), p. 4

The Apostles' Creed

Prayer

O God — Help us keep our faith and trust focused on you. When confronted by mystery, help us to remember that we do not always have to have answers. Deliver us from the fear of what might happen and give us the grace to enjoy what now is. We are not yet willing to put our complete trust in you alone, but we are willing to be made willing. This we pray, and also as you taught us . . .

The Lord's Prayer

Hymn (Sing the last stanza of today's hymn)

The Benediction

The Lord bless you, and keep you.
The Lord make his face shine upon you,
    and be gracious unto you.
The Lord look upon you with favor
    and give you peace;

Overcoming Anxiety and Worry

Welcome/Introductions

Invocation

This is the day which the Lord has made;
let us rejoice and be glad in it. (Psalm 118:24)

Hymn

"God Will Take Care of You"

Text: Mrs. W. Stillman Martin
Tune: Rev. W. Stillman Martin

About the Hymn

Rev. W. Stillman Martin wrote the music for this lovely old hymn. His wife wrote the words.

There is an interesting story regarding the writing of "God Will Take Care of You." Once when Rev. Martin had accepted an invitation to preach at a church in New York City, his wife became ill and was unable to accompany him. He was so concerned about her that he considered canceling the engagement. But his nine-year-old son spoke up saying, "Daddy, don't you think that if God wants you to preach today, he will take care of mother while you are away?"

Martin replied, "Yes, son, I know he will." He kissed his son and wife goodbye and went off to preach. When he returned later, he was happy to find his wife much improved. She gave him a poem she had written while he was gone — one inspired by their son's beautiful faith. He sat down and composed the music.

"God Will Take Care of You" has brought comfort and consolation to millions of people over the years.

Scripture

Therefore I tell you, do not be anxious about your life, what you shall eat or what you shall drink, nor about your body, what you shall put on. Is not life more than food, and the body more than clothing?

— Matthew 6:25

Special Music (If any)

Sermon Seed

Not only Jesus but many wise people have admonished us not to worry so much. We know that in our heads, but how do we get it into our hearts? Here are a couple of quotes to help us try once again:

"Worry affects the circulation — the heart, the glands, the whole nervous system. I have never known a person who died from overwork, but many who died from worry and doubt."

— Dr. Charles Mayo

Don't you trouble trouble
    Till trouble troubles you.
Don't you look for trouble;
    Let trouble look for you.

Don't you hurry worry
    By worrying lest it come.
To flurry is to worry,
    'Twill miss you if you're mum.

If minding will not mend it,
    Then better not to mind;
The best thing is to end it —
    Just leave it all behind.
            — Anonymous

The Apostles' Creed

Prayer

O God — Let us move into each new day with courage, knowing you are by our side. When hope and good cheer fail, carry us through. When confronted by mystery, help us to remember we do not have to know everything. Help us to learn something this day, that we shall be wiser at its close. May we rest our hearts in thee — at least for today. This we pray, and also as you taught us . . .

The Lord's Prayer

Hymn (Sing the last stanza of today's hymn)

The Benediction

May the Lord watch between me and thee when we are absent one from another (Genesis 31:49)

God's Grace

Welcome/Introductions

Invocation

The hour cometh, and now is, when the true worshipers shall worship God in spirit and in truth; for such are the ones God seeks as worshipers. (John 4:23 — adapted)

Hymn

"Amazing Grace"
Text: John Newton (1725-1807)

About the Hymn

John Newton was born in London, July 24, 1725. His father was a sea captain. His mother, a deeply pious woman, though frail in health, found her greatest joy in teaching her son scripture passages and hymns. When he was only four he was able to read the Catechism. His mother often expressed the hope that her son would become a minister.

When he was seven years old, however, Newton's mother died and he was left to shift largely for himself. On his eleventh birthday, his greatest wish came true, and he was able to join his father at sea. His dream soon turned into a nightmare when his father rejected him. He clashed with his employers and finally ended up in jail. Released, he continued a life of wild and immoral living, and for some years served as the captain of a slave ship.

The memory of his mother's teachings and the reading of Thomas A. Kempis' great book, *Imitation of Christ* quickened his conscience. Not until after a terrifying experience in a storm at sea and his deliverance from a malignant fever did he return to his faith and found peace with God.

When he was thirty-nine, he became a minister and served the church until his death at eighty-two. In his later years he would often tell his audiences, "My memory is nearly gone, but I remember two things: that I am a great sinner and that Christ is a great Savior."

It was during his pastorate at Olney, England, that he wrote many of his great hymns. "Amazing Grace" is perhaps the best known of the hymns he wrote, and seems to sum up his own life and gratitude for God's unmerited favor. His tombstone has this inscription, written by Newton before his death in 1807:

> John Newton, clerk, once an Infidel and Libertine, a servant of slavers in Africa, was, by the rich Mercy of our Lord and Saviour Jesus Christ, preserved, restored, pardoned and appointed to preach the faith he had long labored to destroy.

Other hymns by John Newton:
"How Sweet the Name of Jesus Sounds"
"One There Is Above All Others"
"Glorious Things of Thee Are Spoken"

Scripture

For by grace you have been saved through faith; and this is not your own doing, it is the gift of God — not of works, lest any one should boast.

— Ephesians 2:8-9

Special Music (If any)

Sermon Seed

One thing that children do extremely well is, from time to time, give us glimpses of grace. One of the tenderest stories I ever heard deals with children and grace.

When former hostage William F. Keough, Jr. reached Wiesbaden, West Germany, he found tons of letters waiting for him. Keough says he is not likely to forget one of them soon. It said: "I'm Susie Jones. I am eight-years-old. I am in the third grade, so I know what you've been through!"

How spontaneous and understandable for an eight-year-old. Children brighten our world and warm our hearts.

> — *An Encouraging Word*
> by Roger Prescott and
> Ronald Rude
> (C.S.S., 1983), p. 1

The Apostles' Creed

Prayer

O Thou who Thyself art everlasting grace, give us tender hearts toward all those feeling the need of forgiveness. With the grace so freely given to us, let us share it with others. Let the salt of our prayers preserve our humanity. This we pray, and also as you taught us . . .

The Lord's Prayer

Hymn (Sing the last stanza of today's hymn)

The Benediction

May the Lord watch between me and thee when we are absent one from another. (Genesis 31:49)

Love

Welcome/Introductions

Invocation

I was glad when they said unto me, "We will go into the house of the Lord. (Psalm 122:1)

Hymn

"Jesus, Lover of My Soul" (Sing first stanza)
Text: Charles Wesley (1707-1788)

About the Hymn

Charles Wesley (1707-1788) and his brother, John, were reformers and founders of the Methodist Church. Charles was the youngest of nineteen children born to Rev. Samuel and Susannah Wesley. He authored over 6,500 hymns during his lifetime. He wrote while traveling on horseback, often stopping at houses along the way to ask for quill and paper; he wrote love letters in the form of hymns; he wrote a hymn on his wedding day; and as he lay dying, his last words were of a hymn which he dictated to his wife.

Perhaps his most famous and some say his best hymn was "Jesus, Lover of My Soul." No one knows for certain what prompted the writing of this hymn. Some say a bird flew into Wesley's room, seeking refuge and that gave him the idea of flying to the Lord's bosom for protection. Others say it was a terrible storm at sea that motivated him.

Charles Wesley felt the impact of a hymn should be apparent from the beginning. He was not concerned with developing an idea through many verses. His point is usually apparent in the first verse, with the following verses repeating the idea with different word pictures and biblical references. The evangelical emphasis of the Wesleys is seen in all Charles' hymns. He wrote of his personal experience of salvation and the joy which resulted from his conversion.

Other Hymns by Charles Wesley:
  "Hark, the Herald Angels Sing"
  "Love Divine, All Love Excelling"
  "Come, Thou Long Expected Jesus"

Scripture
If I speak in tongues of men and of angels, but have not love, I am a noisy gong or a clanging cymbal . . . So faith, hope, love abide, these three; but the greatest of these is love.
— 1 Corinthians 13: 1, 13

Special Music (If any)

Sermon Seed
Love is important at any age. We try to love as God first loved us.

On November 10, 1979, I buried one of the members of our congregation. She was ninety-four years old. Fiercely independent, she had found it necessary to spend the last years of her life in a nursing care center. It wasn't easy for her at first. The following note was found among her things after her death. It was passed to her from one of the men residents:

Mali, I wish we were young again
so I could be with you
So we could walk to the setting sun
Holding our hands when day is done.

Isn't that great! Isn't that fine! How grand that Mali and her friend could feel a glimpse of real love and friendship even (maybe especially) in their later years.

— Rev. Roger Prescott
Chaplain, Bethany Lutheran Home
Council Bluffs, Iowa
Adapted from his book, *An Encouraging Word* (C.S.S., 1983)

Love is a word —
a shameless ragged
ghost of a word —
begging at all doors
for life at any price.
— Eugene O'Neill

The Apostles' Creed

Prayer

God of love, pry us loose from those marginal causes to
which we give ourselves so freely. Glue us to those which show
and share your love. This we pray, and also as you taught us
. . .

The Lord's Prayer

Hymn (Sing the last stanza of today's hymn)

The Benediction

May God bless you and keep you.
May God's face shine on you
    and be gracious to you.
May God look upon you with favor and
    give you peace.

Prayer

Welcome/Introductions

Invocation

This is the day which the Lord has made;
let us rejoice and be glad in it. (Psalm 118:24)

Hymn

"Sweet Hour of Prayer" (Sing first stanza)
Text: William Walford
Tune: William Bradbury

About the Hymn

William Walford was an English layman who owned a small trinket shop in Coleshill, England. He often served as a guest preacher in churches in the area. One day in 1842, a friend stopped in his shop and Walford asked him to write down a poem he had just completed — the words to "Sweet Hour of Prayer." The reason Walford had asked his friend to write down his poem, was that he was blind. He had many reasons to know that an hour spent in communion with God is truly a "sweet hour of prayer."

Three years later, the friend took the poem to New York and it was published in the *New York Observer.* It was not until fourteen years later, however, that anything dramatic happened to these lovely lines. It was in 1859 that William Bradbury set the poem to music. It was soon discovered by millions.

Scripture

He was praying in a certain place, and when he ceased, one of his disciples said to him, "Lord, teach us to pray, as John taught his disciples." And he said to them, "When you pray, say: Father, hallowed be thy name . . ."

— Luke 11:1-2

Special Music (If any)

Sermon Seed

To begin to pray — or to continue — we don't need to know a whole lot about prayer. We don't even need to know a great deal about God. We will learn as we go. Walt Whitman once prayed to "You whoever you are." Of course he lived before Alcoholics Anonymous was founded. One of the A.A. steps of recovery echoes this thought: "We made a decision to turn our will and our lives over to the care of God *as we understood him.*" (Step three)

God has given us a model prayer. One we can use always. Not only is it a model and guide for our prayers, it broadens the horizon of our lives because . . .

You cannot pray the Lord's prayer and
    even once say "I."
You cannot pray the Lord's prayer and
    even once say "My."

Nor can you pray the Lord's prayer and
    not pray for one another,
And when you ask for daily bread,
    you must include your brother.

For others are included . . . in
    each and every plea,
From the beginning to the end of it,
    It does not once say "Me."
        — From a card from
        The Omaha Home for boys

The Apostles' Creed

Prayer

O Eternal God — we pray for faith to take no anxious thought for tomorrow, but to believe in the continuance of Thy past mercies. We come to Thee with the faith that we have. We believe Thou art there and that our seeking will be blessed. Come, Holy Spirit, and fill our hearts with love. This we pray and also as you taught us . . .

The Lord's Prayer

Hymn (Sing the last stanza of today's hymn)

The Benediction

Go in peace and serve the Lord.

Faith

Welcome/Introductions

Invocation
I lift up my eyes to the hills. From whence does my help come?
My help comes from the Lord, who made heaven and earth.
(Psalm 121: 1-2)

Hymn
"My Faith Looks up to Thee"
Text: Ray Palmer (1808-1887)
Tune: Lowell Mason (1792-1872)

About the Hymn
"My Faith Looks up to Thee" is often called America's finest Christian hymn. It was composed by Ray Palmer, a direct descendant of John Adams and his wife, Priscilla.

Poverty forced Palmer to leave home at the age of thirteen and he clerked in a Boston dry good store. It was during this time he passed through several deep spiritual experiences and became a devoted Christian. Friends recognized his unusual gifts and urged him to attend school. Eventually he graduated from Phillips Andover Academy and from Yale University. He taught for several years in New York and New Haven. In 1935, he was ordained to the Congregational ministry.

While he was in New York, he wrote the poem that was to make him famous. He was only twenty-two at the time and had no idea of composing a hymn for general use. He said his poem was the expression of what he was feeling and used it often for his own devotions.

Lowell Mason, a famous musician, came to Palmer years later, after he had established a reputation as a poet, and asked him if he had a poem to be included in a songbook Mason was compiling. Palmer gave him "My Faith Looks up to Thee." Later, Mason said to him, "Mr. Palmer, you may leave many good things, but I think you will be best known to posterity as the author of this beautiful hymn.''

Mason's tune, ''Olivet'' contributed as much to the hymn's beauty as did the words and they have been used together for over 100 years.

Other Hymns by Ray Palmer
''Jesus, These Eyes Have Never Seen''

Other Hymns by Lowell Mason
''May We Your Precepts, Lord, Fulfill''

Scripture
When I look at your heavens, the work of your fingers, the moon and the stars which you have established; what are human beings that you are mindful of them, and mortals that you care for them?

— Psalm 8:3-4

Special Music (If any)

Sermon Seed
Richard Anderson relates a marvelous story of faith:

The six-month night at the South Pole must have seemed endless to Admiral Richard E. Byrd, even though he had provided himself with a small hut and all the necessities of life. One day he wandered away into a snowstorm. Suddenly he realized he could no longer see the smokestack of his little home. What to do? First he determined not to panic. Second, he decided to mark the spot so that he didn't wander off farther into the wrong direction. He hammered a stake into the ice, attached a long rope to it, and then in ever-widening circles moved out toward the peg until he got so far out he almost pulled the peg loose. He went back, refastened it in the ice, and added another section of rope. This time as he circled around the peg he walked directly into the door of his little hut. He had found his way.

We can learn from that. No matter how far we may have wandered on our own, when we become firmly attached to Christ by a faith that holds on tenaciously, we will find our way through life with the Savior's leading.

> — Richard Anderson/Donald Defner
> *For Example*
> (Concordia Publishing House, 1977) pp. 86-87

The Apostles' Creed

Prayer

We give thanks, O God, for the faith that sustains us. By this faith we try to go where you have called us — like Abel, Enoch, Abraham and Sarah. May this gift of faith be nurtured and cared for by all — and may it take away our sorrow and grant us joy. This we pray, and also as you taught us . . .

The Lord's Prayer

Hymn (Sing the last stanza of today's hymn)

The Benediction

The Lord bless you and keep you.
The Lord make God's face shine on you
    and be gracious to you.
The Lord look upon you with favor and
    give you peace.

The Cross

Welcome/Introductions

Invocation
I lift up my eyes to the hills. From whence does my help come?
My help comes from the Lord, who made heaven and earth.
(Psalm 121: 1-2)

Hymn
"When I Survey the Wondrous Cross" (Sing first stanza)
Text: Isaac Watts (1674-1748)

About the Hymn
Isaac Watts (1674-1748) was a pioneer in the new form of musical worship. He contended that hymns should express Christian faith in the same way that the Psalms expressed Jewish faith.

He also demonstrated that there was a generation gap as far back as the seventeenth century. Even in childhood, Isaac had shown a passion for poetry, rhyming even everyday conversation. His serious-minded father, after several warnings, decided to spank the rhyming nonsense out of his son. But even then Isaac could not resist and pleaded:

"O father, do some pity take
and I will no more verses make."

The world is fortunate that Isaac Watts did not keep this impromptu promise.

When teen-aged, Isaac complained to his father about the dull and monotonous way the Psalms were sung, his father became angry and said, "Well, young man, if you are smarter than King David, why don't you try to write something better." Young Watts accepted the challenge and wrote a hymn which was sung at the service the following Sunday evening. It met with such favorable response that he continued to write hymns every week. Eventually, he wrote more than 600 hymns, including such favorites as: "O God, our Help in Ages Past," and "Joy to the World."

Another great English hymn writer, James Montgomery, has called him "the inventor of hymns in our language." And E. E. Ryden calls "When I Survey the Wondrous Cross" the "Pearl of English hymnody."

Miss Elizabeth Singer was attracted to him by his poetry. When she met him she was greatly disillusioned by his appearance. She turned down his proposal for marriage. Watts remained a bachelor. In 1712 he accepted an invitation to spend a week at the country estate of his friend Sir Thomas Abney. He went for a week but stayed for thirty-six years. He died there in 1748.

Scripture

But far be it from me to glory except in the cross of our Lord Jesus Christ, by which the world has been crucified to me, and I to the world.

— Galatians 6:14

Special Music (If any)

Sermon Seed

In his book, *God's Way*, Harrison Ray Anderson tells this story: One evening, in the little town of Dunscore, Scotland, Carlyle was walking with his friend Ralph Waldo Emerson. They came to a place where the evening sun turned the cross on the village church into a golden color. They stopped. "Look," said Carlyle, "Christ died on the cross, and that built yon church, and that brought you and me together."

Someone has called the cross "The great plus sign of history." Maybe so. For me, it signifies a great intersection. The vertical shaft speaks about divine forgiveness and God's relationship to us. The horizontal shaft speaks about our relationship to each other here on earth. The cross spells out in symbol the "love-God-love-your-neighbor" injunction in the Bible.

Winston Churchill paid a tribute to the young men of the Royal Air Force, who flew to defend England in World War II." Never in the history of the world have so many owed so much to so few." When we think of the cross of Christ, we say: "Never in the history of the universe has humankind owed so much to one."

The Apostles' Creed

Prayer

Spirit of the living God, and promised gift of our savior Jesus Christ, we open now our hearts to receive thee anew. When we survey thy wondrous cross, help us to enlarge our sense of belonging. Renew our joy to the end that our lives may point toward thy cross, that others may be directed to it, and know that thou art love. This we pray, and also as you taught us . . .

The Lord's Prayer

Hymn (Sing the last stanza of today's hymn)

The Benediction

May God bless you and keep you.
May God's face shine on you
    and be gracious to you.
May God look upon you with favor and
    give you peace.

Community/Partnership

Welcome/Introductions

Invocation
This is the day which the Lord has made;
let us rejoice and be glad in it. (Psalm 118:24)

Hymn
"Blest Be the Tie That Binds" (Sing first stanza)
Text: John Fawcett (1740-1817)
Tune: Lowell Mason (1792-1872)

About the Hymn
   John Fawcett (1740-1817) was a Baptist preacher in a small village in England, who never earned more than $100 a year. His family, however, grew and grew. When he was offered a position in a larger church in London, he eagerly made preparations to leave. As they prepared to leave, packing their belongings onto a wagon, they said their good-byes. Fawcett and his wife found they had many bonds with the parish. He preached one final sentiment-laden sermon on his final Sunday. Tears and sighs of the parishioners convinced the Fawcetts that they should stay and continue their ministry where they were. This experience prompted him to write the hymn "Blest Be the Tie That Binds" a short time later.
   The tune is by Lowell Mason.

Other Hymns by John Fawcett
   "Lord, Dismiss Us With Thy Blessing"
   "How Precious is the Book Divine"
   "Praise to Thee, Thou Great Creator"

Other Hymns by Lowell Mason
   "My Faith Looks up to Thee"
   "From Greenland's Icy Mountains"
   "May We Your Precepts, Lord Fulfill"

Scripture

I thank my God in all my remembrance of you, always in every prayer of mine for you all making my prayer with joy, thankful for your partnership in the gospel from the first day until now.

— Philippians 1:3-5

Special Music (If any)

Sermon Seed

A marvelous story about living in "community" that speaks to me about how we can care for each other follows:

For almost a year, an eighty-year-old man made a daily twenty-mile trip to be with his wife, who was in a nursing home. The trip involved about two hours of bus travel each way, but he didn't mind. Always warm and outgoing, he had struck up a friendship with the bus driver and enjoyed the company of other passengers.

One day, he was standing at the bus stop in a pouring rain when a little Volkswagon pulled up and a young man called out that he had come to take him home. He went on to explain that the bus had broken down and that the driver, a friend of his, had phoned to ask if he would go to that bus stop and see that the elderly man waiting there got home safely.

Isn't that kind of helping a beautiful thing?
— From: *An Encouraging Word*
Roger Prescott and Ronald Rude
(C.S.S. Publishing Co., 1983), p. 78

The Apostles' Creed

Prayer

Spirit of the living God — we open our
hearts now to receive thee anew.
Enlarge our expectations —
Deepen our sense of belonging —
And renew our joy to the end that we
    may shine as lights in a darkened world
    and make it easier for others to know
    that thou art love.
Thank you for the tie that binds.
This we pray, and also as you taught us . . .

The Lord's Prayer

Hymn (Sing the last stanza of today's hymn)

The Benediction

The Lord bless you and keep you.
The Lord make his face to shine upon you
    and be gracious to you.
The Lord look upon you with favor and
    give you peace.

Friendship

Welcome/Introductions

Invocation

This is the day which the Lord has made;
let us rejoice and be glad in it. (Psalm 118:24)

Hymn

"What a Friend We Have in Jesus" (Sing first stanza)
Text: Joseph Scriven
Tune: Charles Converse

About the Hymn

The writer of this moving hymn was Joseph Scriven. Born in 1819 in Dublin, Ireland, he was educated at Trinity College in that city.

Early in life he discovered how much he needed the friendship of Christ. The Irish lass to whom he was married, accidentally and tragically drowned on the even of their wedding.

He moved to Port Hope, Ontario, Canada, when he was twenty-five. He worked with the poor and underprivileged.

His mother, back home in Ireland, whom he had not seen for ten years, became ill and he was unable to return to be with her. He produced this poem and sent it to her hoping that it would remind her of her always-present friend, Jesus Christ.

The words were eventually seen by a German-American lawyer and composer, Charles Converse. He wrote the music to Scriven's three verses and the world was blessed by this popular and nourishing hymn.

Scriven's second fiance died after a brief illness, so he lived and died as a lonely man. The poem he wrote to comfort his mother has brought comfort to millions.

Scripture

This is my commandment, that you love one another as I have loved you. Greater love has no one than this, that one lay down one's life for a friend. You are my friends if you do what I command you. No longer do I call you servants, for the servant does not know what the master is doing; but I have called you friends, for all that I have heard from God I have made known to you.

— John 15:12-15
An Inclusive-Language Lectionary

Special Music (If any)

Sermon Seed

Friendship may be the highest relationship on earth. Not everyone is lucky enough to have a mate. Not everyone can have brothers and sisters. But everyone can have — and be —. a friend.

We need to be friends with:

1. Ourselves (Luke 10:27)
2. Others (John 15:15)
3. Nature (Psalm 24:1)

The importance of friendship is reflected in this 200-year-old poem:

The world is so empty
if one thinks only
of mountains, rivers, and
cities; but to know someone
who thinks and feels with me,
and who, though distant
is close to me in spirit,
this makes the earth for me
an inhabited garden.

— Johann Wolfgang von Goethe
(1749-1832)

The Apostles' Creed

Prayer

O God — we thank you for this great and mysterious opportunity called life. Be our guard against all that would bring us low. Gladden our hearts with friends and good conversation; and surround us with love that we may be free to truly live. This we pray, and also as you taught us . . .

The Lord's Prayer

Hymn (Sing the last stanza of today's hymn)

The Benediction

The Lord bless you and keep you.
The Lord make God's face to shine on you
    and be gracious to you.
The Lord look upon you with favor and
    give you peace.

Index of Scripture

Acknowledgements

Grateful acknowledgement is made to the following:

An Encouraging Word by Roger Prescott and Ronald Rude, Copyright 1983, C.S.S. Publishing Company. Used by permission.

Deep in December by Gerhard E. Frost, Copyright 1986, Logos Art Productions, 6160 Carmen Ave. East, Inver Grove Heights, MN 55076. Used by permission.

For Example by Richard Anderson and Donald Defner, Copyright 1977, Concordia Publishing House. Used by permission from CPH.

Hello, My Friend by Roger Prescott, Copyright 1981, C.S.S. Publishing Company. Used by permission.

Kept Moments by Gerhard E. Frost, Winston Press, Copyright 1982, Mrs. Gerhard E. Frost. Used by permission of Mrs. Gerhard E. Frost.

Lord's Prayer Card, Omaha Home for Boys. Used by permission.

This Land of Leaving by Gerhard E. Frost, Copyright 1986, Logos Art Productions, 6160 Carmen Ave. East, Inver Grove Heights, MN 55076. Used by permission.

About the Authors

Roger K. Prescott is Chaplain of Bethany Lutheran Home in Council Bluffs, Iowa. A graduate of the University of Minnesota and Luther Northwestern Theological Seminary, Prescott speaks words of warmth and encouragement through his sermons, talks, telephone ministry (called Warmline), his counseling and his writing.

He recently was accepted into the College of Chaplains of the American Protestant Health Association.

He runs a little and writes a little each day, currently dealing with the themes of aging, grief, and well-being. Prescott is a retired U.S. Naval Reserve Chaplain. This is his seventh book.

Shirley M. Prescott has been married to Roger for 36 years, during which time they have worked together in their home as parents of four children and in the parish as facilitators of adult study and friendship groups. Shirley is secretary for the Pastoral Care Department at Immanuel Medical Center, Omaha, Nebraska.